Big Machines

Big Machines Fly!

Catherine Veitch

Heinemann

LIBRARY

Chicago, Illinois

Edited by Helen Cox Cannons and Kathryn Clay
Designed by Tim Bond and Peggie Carley
Picture research by Mica Brancic and Tracy Cummins
Production by Helen McCreath
Originated by Capstone Global Library Ltd
Printed and bound in China by Leo Paper Group

18 17 16 15 14
10 9 8 7 6 5 4 3 2 1

Cataloging-in-publication information is on file
with the Library of Congress.
ISBN 978-1-4846-0586-8 (Hardcover)
ISBN 978-1-4846-0593-6 (eBook PDF)

Photo Credits
Alamy: © Antony Nettle, 12, 13, © CRG Design, 20, © one-image
photography, 21;Getty Images: AFP/Eric Feferberg, 9 inset,
Stocktrek Images, 4, 5, 22a; Library of Congress Prints and
Photographs Division: Bain News Service, 7 inset; NASA:
14, 15, 16 inset, 16, 17, 18, 19, 22c, back cover, Carla Thomas,
19 inset; Shutterstock: Atlaspix, front cover, Charles Shapiro,
8, 9, 22b, gary yim, 6, 7, Steve Mann, 10, 11, 22d, back cover

Every effort has been made to contact copyright holders
of material reproduced in this book. Any omissions will
be rectified in subsequent printings if notice is given to
the publisher.

All the Internet addresses (URLs) given in this book were
valid at the time of going to press. However, due to the
dynamic nature of the Internet, some addresses may have
changed, or sites may have changed or ceased to exist
since publication. While the author and publisher regret
any inconvenience this may cause readers, no responsibility
for any such changes can be accepted by either the author
or the publisher.

Contents

Cargo Jets. 4

Hot Air Balloons. 6

Airships. 8

Chinooks. 10

Super Jumbo. 12

Space Station. 14

Rockets. 16

Space Shuttle. 18

Sizing Things Up 20

Quiz. 22

Glossary 23

Find Out More. 24

Index. 24

Some words are shown in bold, **like this.** You can find out what they mean by looking in the glossary.

Cargo Jets

These planes don't carry passengers. Their large rear doors open to easily load **cargo**.

Even full-size vehicles fit on these large jets.

Hot Air Balloons

Hot air balloons use air to fly. A flame heats up the air that **expands** the balloon. Riders stand in a basket called a **gondola**.

gondola

Hot air balloons are sometimes shaped like fun objects, like this chicken balloon.

The first hot air balloon
was flown in 1783.

Airships

A gas called **helium** is blown into an airship to make it fly. It's just like blowing up a balloon!

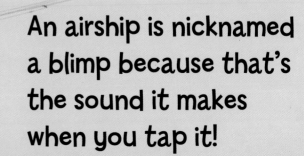

An airship is nicknamed a blimp because that's the sound it makes when you tap it!

Drivers and passengers sit in a
cabin underneath the airship.

Chinooks

The Chinook is a large helicopter. It carries **troops** and supplies to battlefields.

The Chinook has two sets of spinning **rotor blades**. Most helicopters only have one.

Chinooks have two engines. If one engine stops working, the helicopter can still fly with just one engine.

Super Jumbo

This **double-decker** is the largest passenger plane in the world. More than 800 people fit on its two floors.

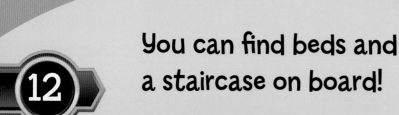

You can find beds and a staircase on board!

Super

Big

Mighty

Size

Space Station

Astronauts live and work at the *International Space Station.*

The space station is moving
around Earth all the time.
It circles Earth once every
90 minutes!

Rockets

Rockets helped to **propel** space shuttles into space.

The Saturn V rocket weighed as much as 400 elephants.

Super

Big

Mighty

Size

The Saturn V rocket helped transport the first astronauts on the Moon.

Space Shuttle

A space shuttle carried astronauts into space and back again.

Two huge rockets blasted the shuttle into space.

Space shuttles didn't use engine power to return to Earth. They **glided** back down.

Sizing Things Up

Super Jumbo

Four engines
Two levels
Holds 853 passengers
Wingspan............. 262 feet (80 meters)
Speed................ up to 560 miles
(901 kilometers) per hour

Boeing 737

Two engines
One level
Holds 215 passengers
Wingspan . . . . 113 feet (34 meters)
Speed . . . . up to 583 miles
(938 kilometers) per hour

Quiz

How much of a Machine Mega-Brain are you?
Can you match each machine name to its correct photo?

**space station • airship
Chinook • cargo jet**

1

2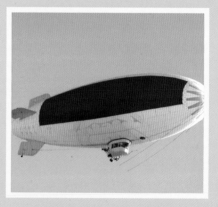

3

4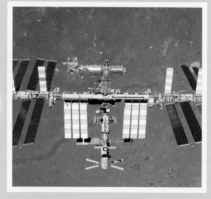

Check the answers on the opposite page
to see if you got all four correct.

Glossary

astronaut a crew member of a spacecraft

cargo objects carried by a ship, aircraft, or other vehicle

double-decker a vehicle with two floors

expand to grow larger

glide to move without any effort

gondola the part of an airship in which the crew travels

helium a lightweight, colorless gas that does not burn

propel to move forward

rotor blade a part of a machine with a sharp edge that spins

troop a group of soilders

Find Out More

Books

Abramovitz, Melissa. *Military Airplanes*. Military Machines. Mankato, Minn.: Capstone Press, 2012.

Goldish, Meish. *Freaky-Big Airplanes*. World's Biggest. New York: Bearport, 2010.

Websites

airandspace.si.edu/explore-and-learn/topics/shuttle.cfm
kids.discovery.com/tell-me/machines/amazing-aircraft

Index

A
airships 8, 9
astronauts 14, 17, 18
B
blimps 8, 9
Boeing 737s 21
C
cargo 4
cargo jets 4, 5
Chinooks 10, 11

E
engines 11, 19, 20, 21
H
helium 8
hot air balloons 6, 7
P
passengers 4, 6, 9, 12, 20, 21
R
rockets 16, 17, 18
rotor blades 10

S
Saturn V 16, 17
space shuttles 16, 18, 19
space stations 14, 15
super jumbos 12, 20